# Mindful Meandering

*132 Original Continuous-Line Quilting Designs*

## Laura Lee Fritz

C&T PUBLISHING

Text copyright © 2008 by Laura Lee Fritz

Artwork copyright © 2008 by C&T Publishing, Inc.

Publisher: *Amy Marson*

Editorial Director: *Gailen Runge*

Acquisitions Editor: *Jan Grigsby*

Editor: *Stacy Chamness*

Technical Editor: *Stacy Chamness, Georgie Gerl*

Proofreader: *Wordfirm Inc.*

Cover Designer/Book Designer: *Christina Jarumay*

Junior Designer: *Kerry Graham*

Production Coordinator: *Matt Allen*

Illustrator: *Richard Sheppard*

Photography by Luke Mulks and Diane Pedersen of C&T Publishing unless otherwise noted

Published by C&T Publishing, Inc., P.O. Box 1456, Lafayette, CA 94549

Library of Congress Cataloging-in-Publication Data

Fritz, Laura Lee.

 Mindful meandering : 132 original continuous-line quilting designs / Laura Lee Fritz.

  p. cm.

 ISBN 978-1-57120-507-0 (paper trade : alk. paper)

 1. Quilting. 2. Quilts--Design. I. Title.

 TT835.F7575 2008

 746.46'041--dc22

     2007024744

Printed in the United States of America

10 9 8 7 6 5 4

# Contents

# What You Can Do With These Designs

## What You Can Do With These Designs

Add beauty and special meaning to your quilting projects by using the graceful continuous-line images shown in the following pages. Whether you are quilting by hand, home sewing machine, or with a long-arm machine, this collection of designs will be a generous resource library. Combine them with each other and with interesting background-filling textures. Enlarge or reduce any of the designs to use on your quilts, and feel free to arrange and combine these ideas with more of your own.

## Planning the Design

If you think of your quilt in terms of a stage, and the quilting designs as the actors on that stage, designing your overall quilting plan will be easy. One design will act as the lead character on center stage, with a supporting cast of one or more secondary design ideas. Provide some backdrops, such as a background grid and some architecture, and your story will unfold.

"Transparent" designs combine interesting shapes but they are not made up of recognizable imagery. An overall meandering is an example. Because of their simplicity, transparent designs don't jump out at you as you study a quilt. You can combine recognizable images with transparent designs, such as an oak leaf "floating" in still waters. The Mindful Meanderings include some of these totally transparent designs, and some combination imagery/transparent texture designs.

# Transferring Designs

If you aren't ready to make the leap into free-motion quilting, there are simple methods to transfer the designs onto your quilt top.

## Paper or Tulle

Trace the designs onto paper with a black permanent pen so you can use a copy machine to resize any image for your block or border. Trace the tracing again onto stencil plastic and cut it out.

You could alternately trace the design onto tulle.

Both of these methods are a means to draw onto your quilt top with chalk, washout pencil, clean-erase pencil or a water/air soluble pen.

## Water-soluble Stabilizer

You can also trace your designs onto water-soluble stabilizer with a water-soluble pen and quilt through it as the topmost layer of your quilt. Try the Solvy stabilizers made by Sulky, or Dissolve from Superior Threads, as they really do wash out of the cloth.

## Washable Marker

Another option is to trace directly onto your quilt top with a washable marker.

Draw the designs onto paper with a black permanent pen and use a copy machine to resize them for your block or border. Clean white paper and bold black drawing lines will project best through the cloth.

> **Tip**
> *A recycled sliding-window pane (still framed) or glass door panel from a shower enclosure will serve you well as a light table.*

Lay a glass panel over a quilt frame or sawhorse set, place a light source such as a four-foot fluorescent shop light below the "table." Now spread your quilt top on the glass and turn the light on. Slide your drawings under the quilt, and position as desired. Trace these designs directly onto your quilt top with a washable marker.

> **Tip**
> *For a whimsical or a folk-art look, instead of tracing you can draw or quilt freehand, following the design that you have right in front of you.*

# Start Quilting

Practice your machine quilting in order to find your rhythm, and learn to sew at a constant speed.

> **Tip**
> *Warm up by tracing the designs with your fingertips or a pencil to practice the paths. This tracing makes the pattern a physical memory and helps you quilt more smoothly. You may even learn to stitch many of them freehand.*

### Sewing a Continuous-Line Quilting Design

*Note any pattern sections where you change sewing direction, sew over an area twice, or sew over an existing line of stitching. You may find it helpful to draw arrows using a highlighter marker on the pattern to guide you.*

*For most of the patterns the starting and stopping points are indicated. You can start at either end of the pattern and sew left to right or right to left.*

When you start or end a line of quilting, or when your top thread or bobbin is depleted, knot the end(s) of your stitching line and thread a needle with the thread tails. Use a long-eye sharp embroidery needle for the tail so both threads will fit through at once. Try wrapping the pair of threads around the eye tightly, pinch the thread to hold the tiny loops as you withdraw the needle, then slip the eye over these tight little loops. Sew these ends by sliding the needle back along your quilting line, pull the needle out, bury the knot into the batting, and cut the tail.

# Mindful Meandering

## Mindful Meandering

The words **meandering** and **stippling** have become interchangeable catchalls for any scribble pattern done all over a quilt. In truth, these words have individual definitions beyond the vague use they get these days.

A stippled pattern in a pencil-artist's hand is a mass of tiny dots, closer or farther apart, to create an array of gray tones, just like we used to see in newspaper photos before modern newspaper presses. In quilting, it used to mean the smallest possible random stitches, quite truly resembling those dots.

Meandering came into use by machine quilters who needed a word to describe a type of design that wandered all over a quilt without crossing other lines, nor having any other definable form to name the design after. So in fact, it would be an *apparently* random sort of pattern that would be a meandering format. Note my use of the word "apparently"—for in order to appear random, a good design has to have a set of rules.

For instance, my *jigsaw meandering* looks like I'm quilting around a quilt covered with coins. I put into mind whether they are dime-sized or quarter-sized, so I can keep the size consistent from start to finish on the quilt.

1   In Italian, the word for worm is vermicelli. *Vermicelli meandering*
is wiggles that are much longer (thus named for the
entertaining earthworm).

2   *Right-angle meandering* is mostly square angles—
still apparently random, still no crossover lines.

3   Here is my *all-points meander*:

4   My signature meandering combines all four of those.

These meanderings actually only become true stipple designs when
they are created so small that they totally flatten the batting in the quilt.

at follows is a collection of doodles that meander about within a set of rules unique to each. More studied overall designs, which really too identifiable to fit my definition, will follow and even require crossing over lines to get made. I, too, make rules only to break them.

5 | 6

7 | 8

The dogs' eyes are created with a backstitch.

19 | 20

23

32

33

34

Mindful Meandering

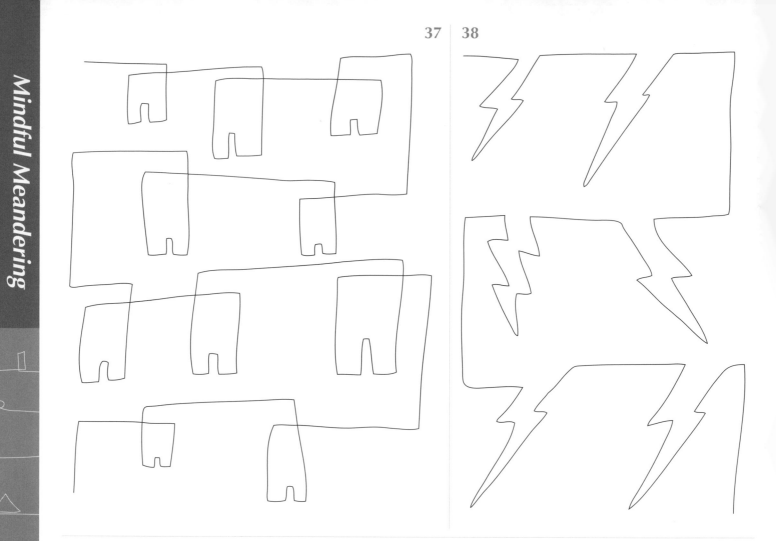

**39**

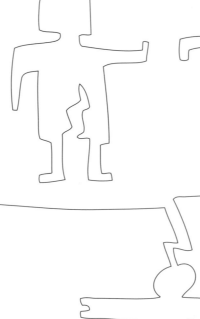

41

42

44

45

48

51

52

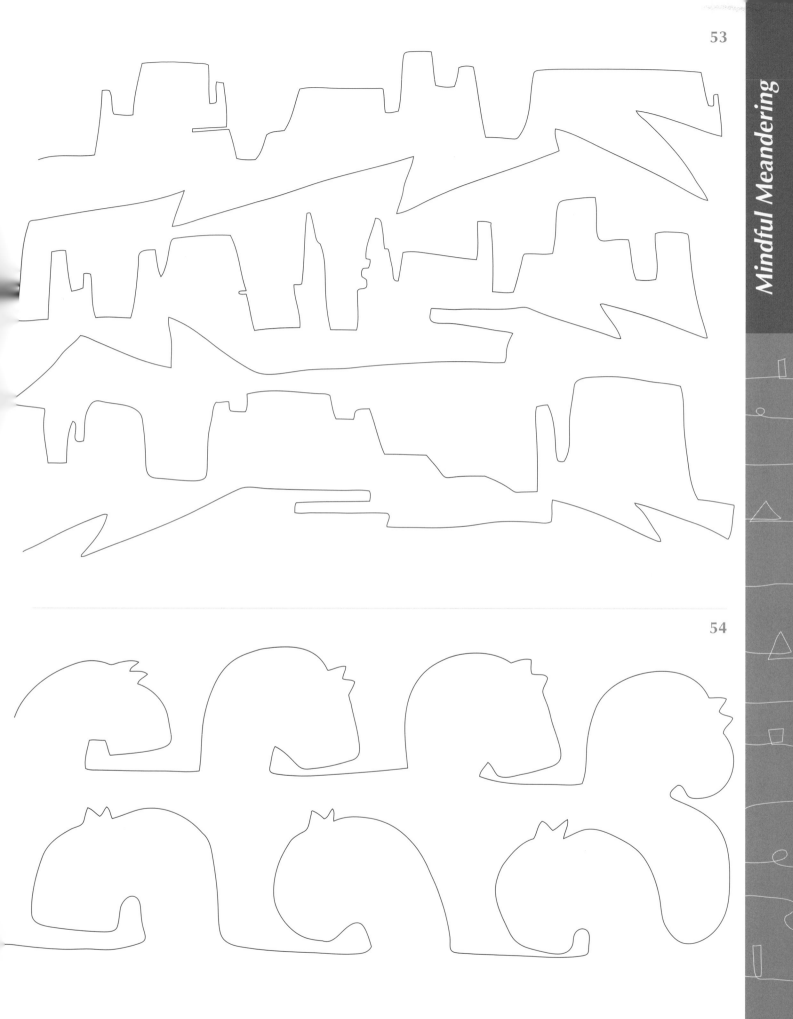

*Mindful Meandering*

59

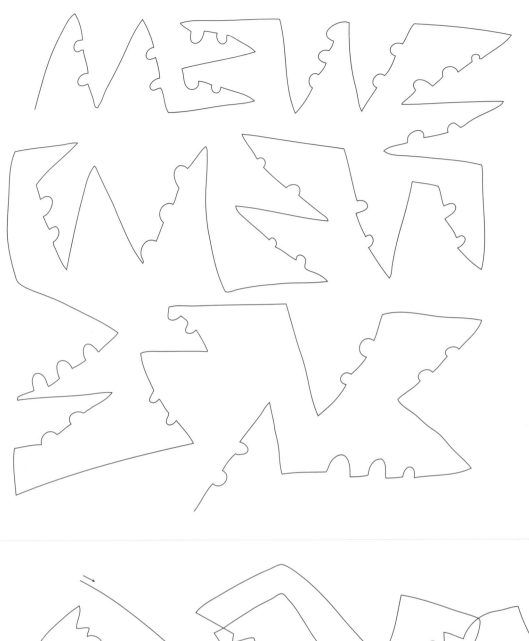

Mindful Meandering

30

68 69

72 | 73

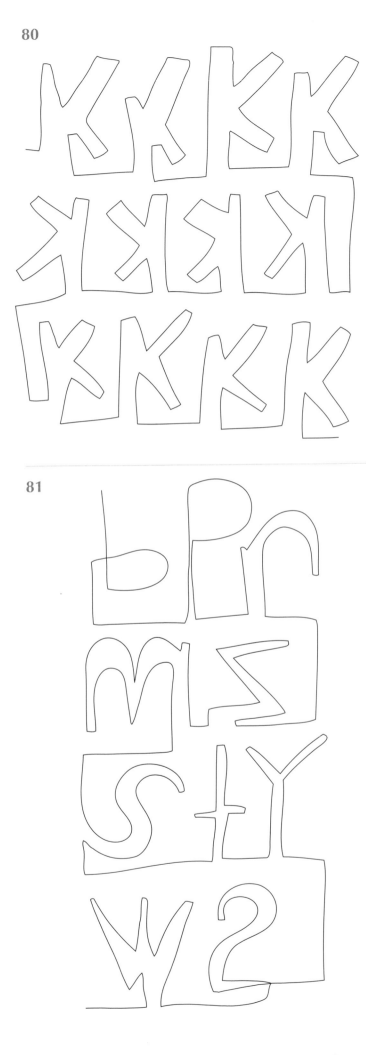

81

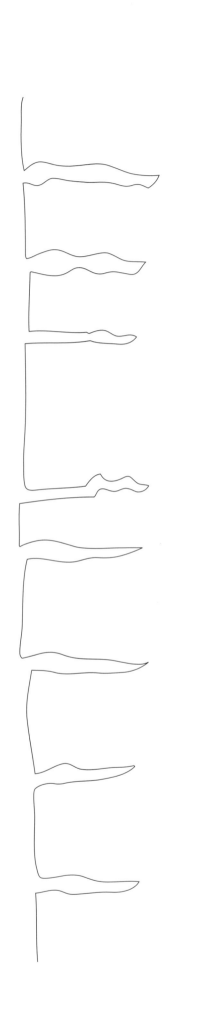

# Square Dancing

## Square Dancing

If you are machine quilting a pattern, you begin to feel and hear the beat of your pattern, like music. The beat moves your body like a dance partner, and when you goof in your pattern, you can tell by a sense of having missed a beat.

Some quilts are made of small squares of the same size—organized, like the trip-around-the-world quilts, or nothing more than a bunch of square scraps. Use the seam lines to guide your design changes . . . create the quilting pattern to play with the grid format.

### Tip
*Stitch slowly when you are entering the thick part of a seam. Seam allowance wads break threads and chip needle tips.*

These designs are drawn on a layout of dots that represent seams, to help you see how the patterns are made in a relationship to the quilt squares. If it helps, take a light-colored pencil and faintly draw in the lines to connect the dots.

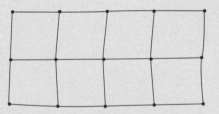

Enjoy combining more than one grid design in a quilt. Trip-around-the-world is fun to add changes to—follow a particular fabric on its path around the center, always doing a design in squares of that fabric unlike what you are doing in any of the other fabrics.

84

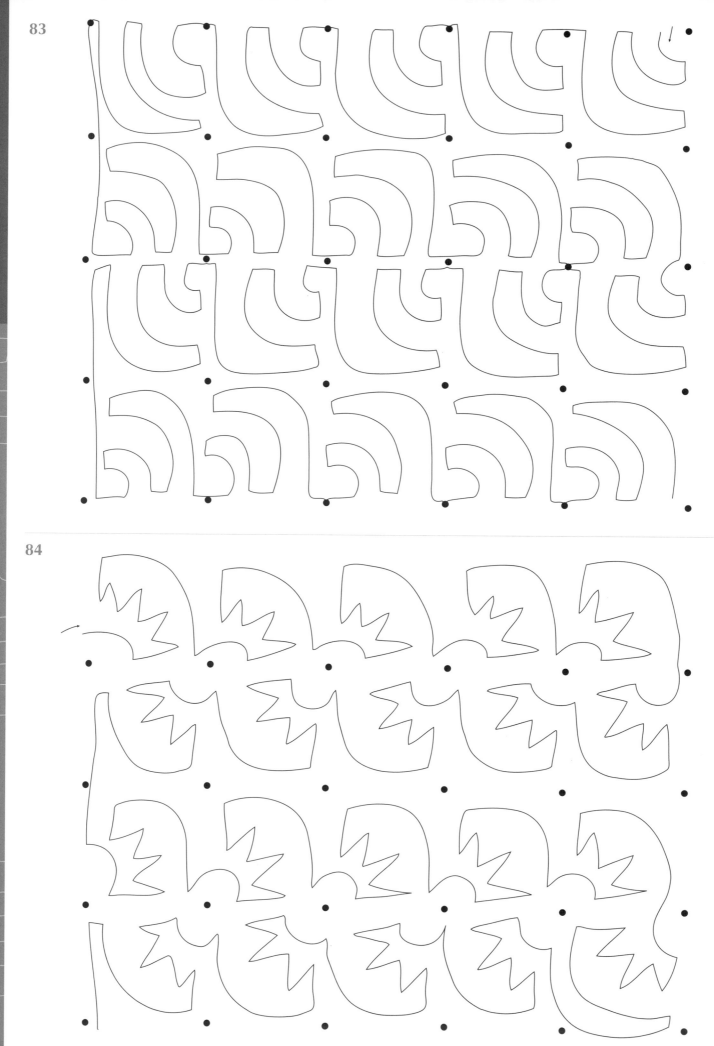

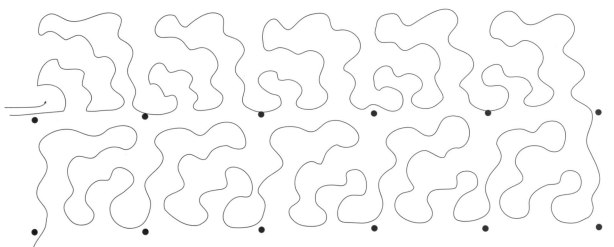

**88**

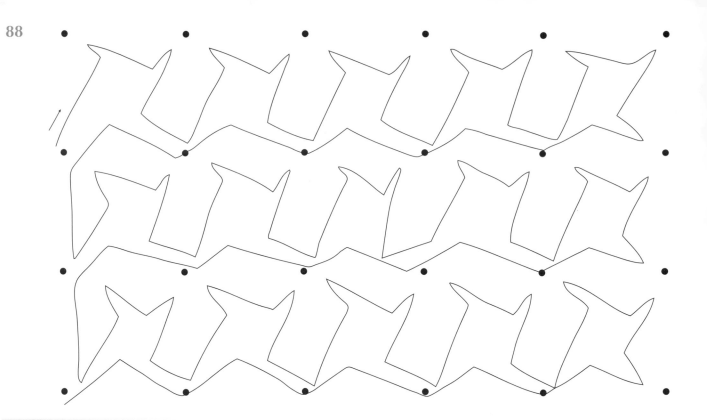

**89**

**90**

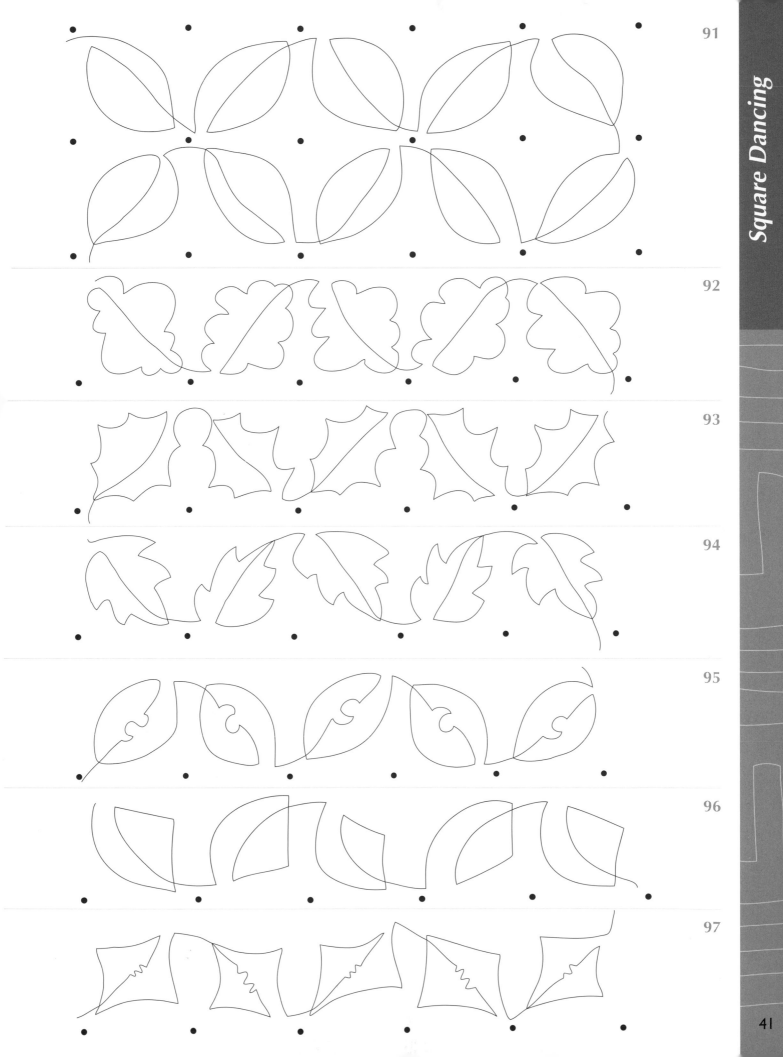

98

99

100

101

102

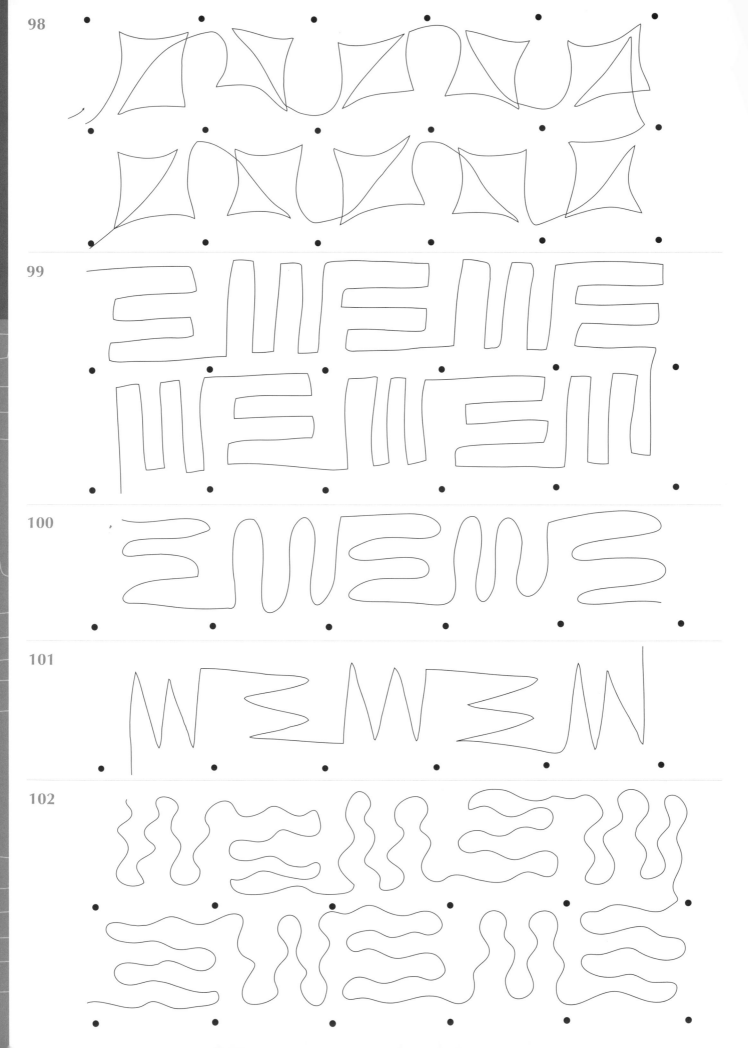

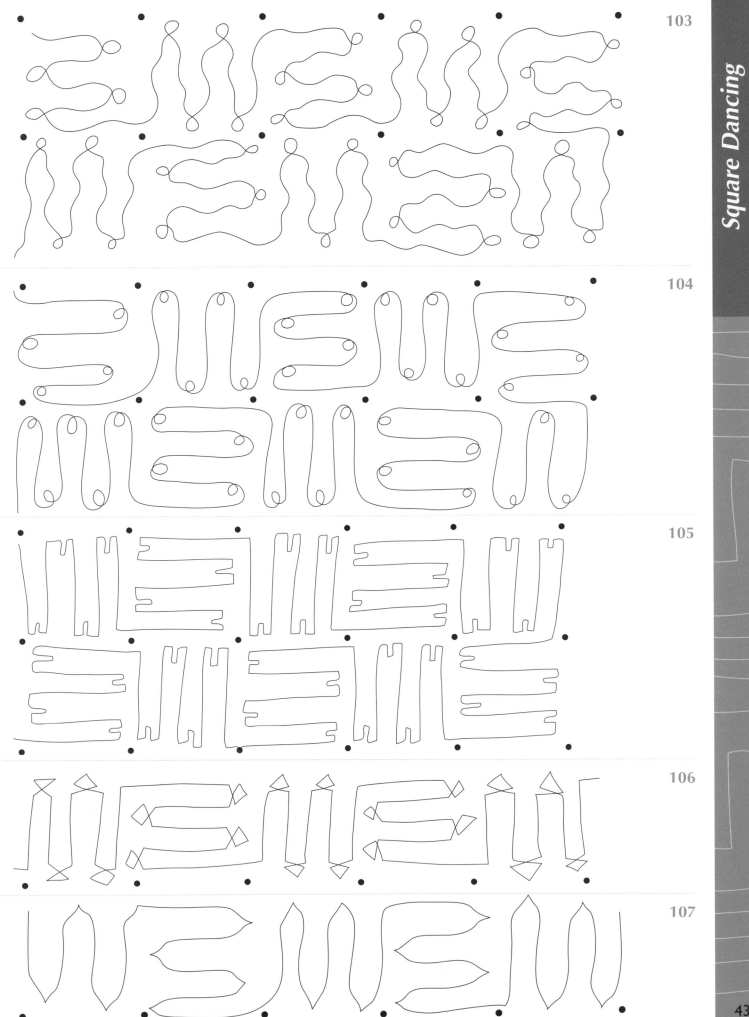

**Square Dancing**

103

104

105

106

107

108

109

110

111

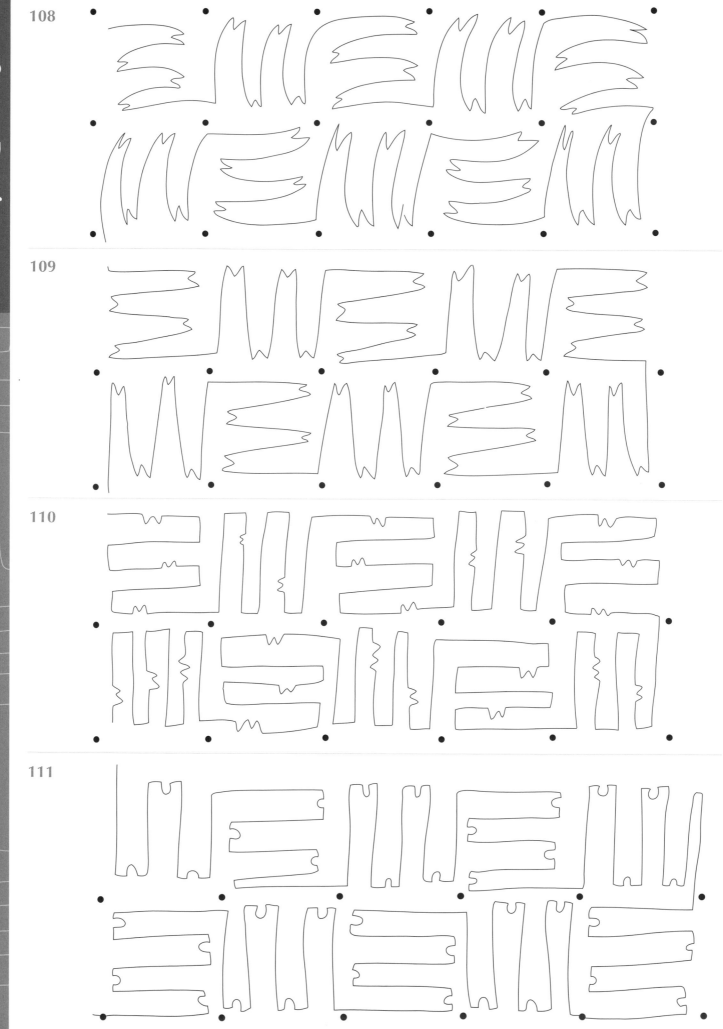

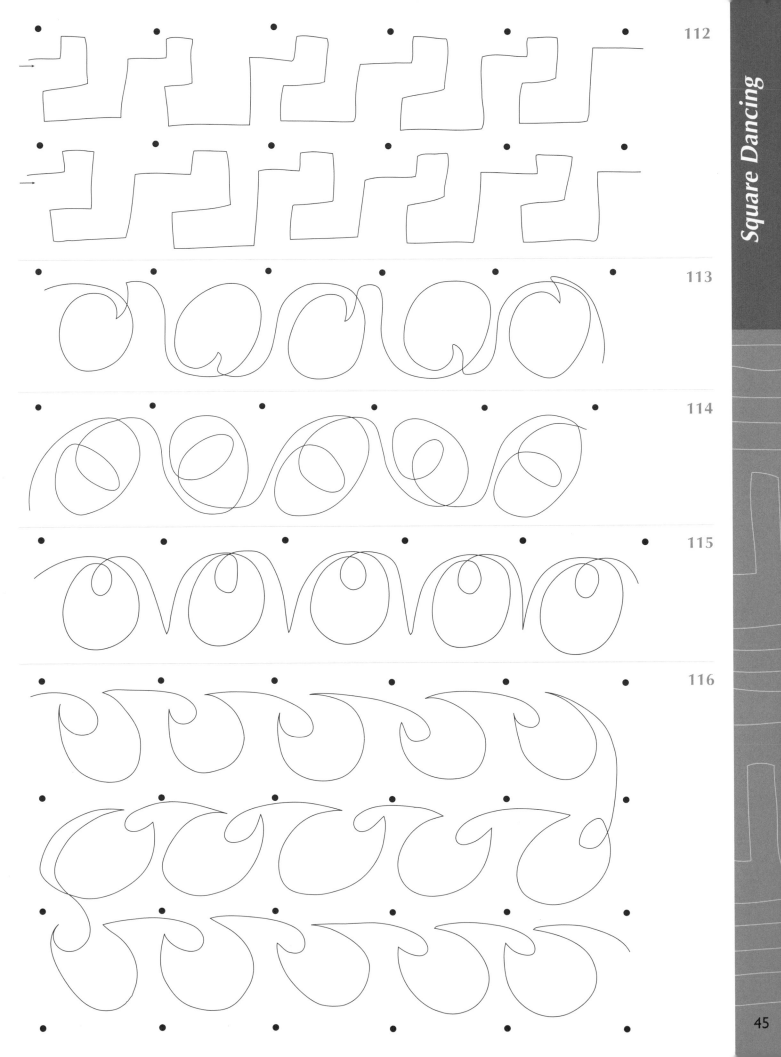

112

113

114

115

116

**117**

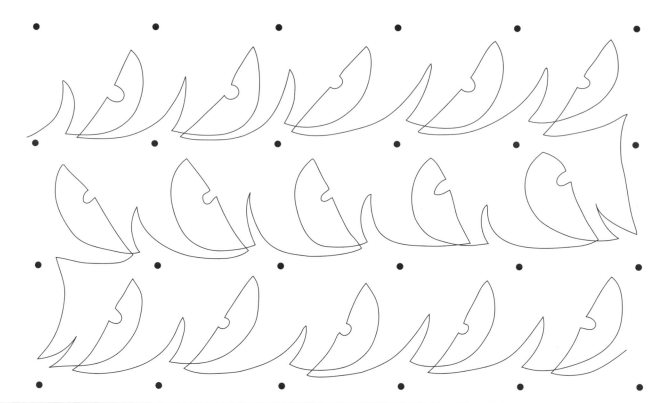

**118**

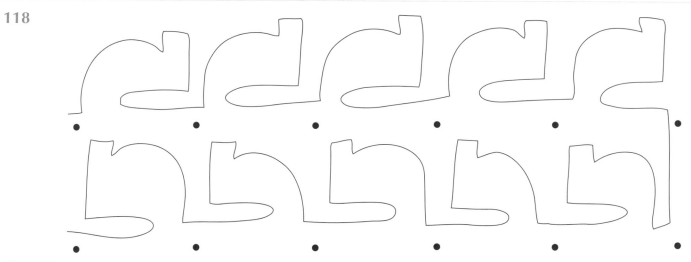

**119**

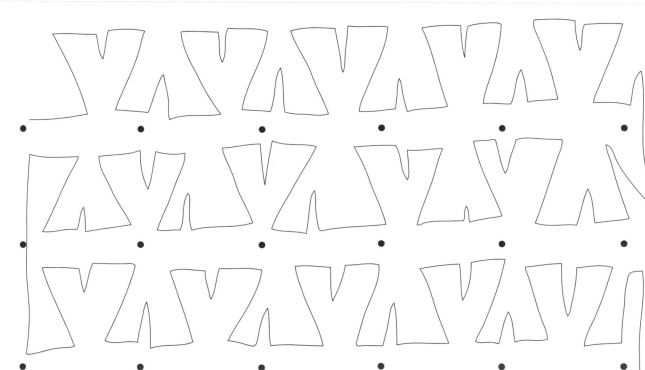

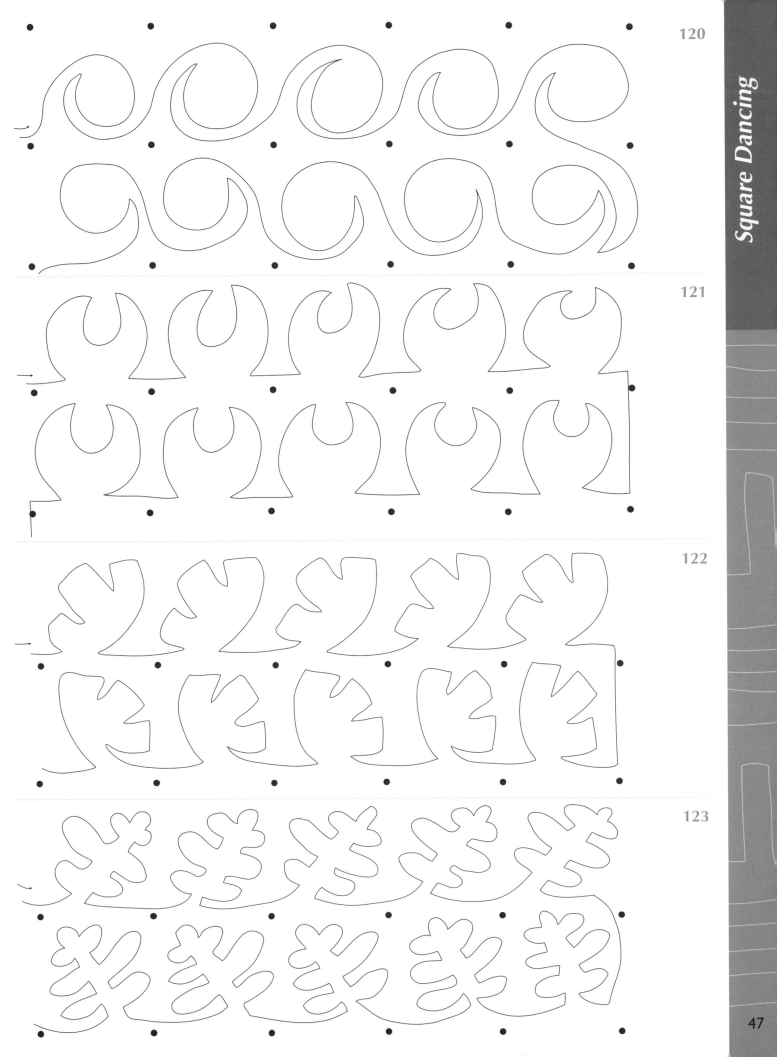

120

121

122

123

# Orange Peel

## Orange Peel

The standard quilt block called Orange Peel makes a terrific pattern for quilting a grid of square blocks. When done carefully, you will get the illusion of interlocking rings, as in the double wedding ring. So many variations are possible that I can call the Orange Peel a format for design, not just a pattern.

Here is the Orange Peel format:

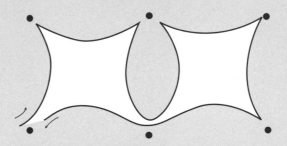

- Start in the lower left.
- Draw the same line around 3 sides.
- The next "row" completes the bottom of the design.
- Dance *around* the seam points!

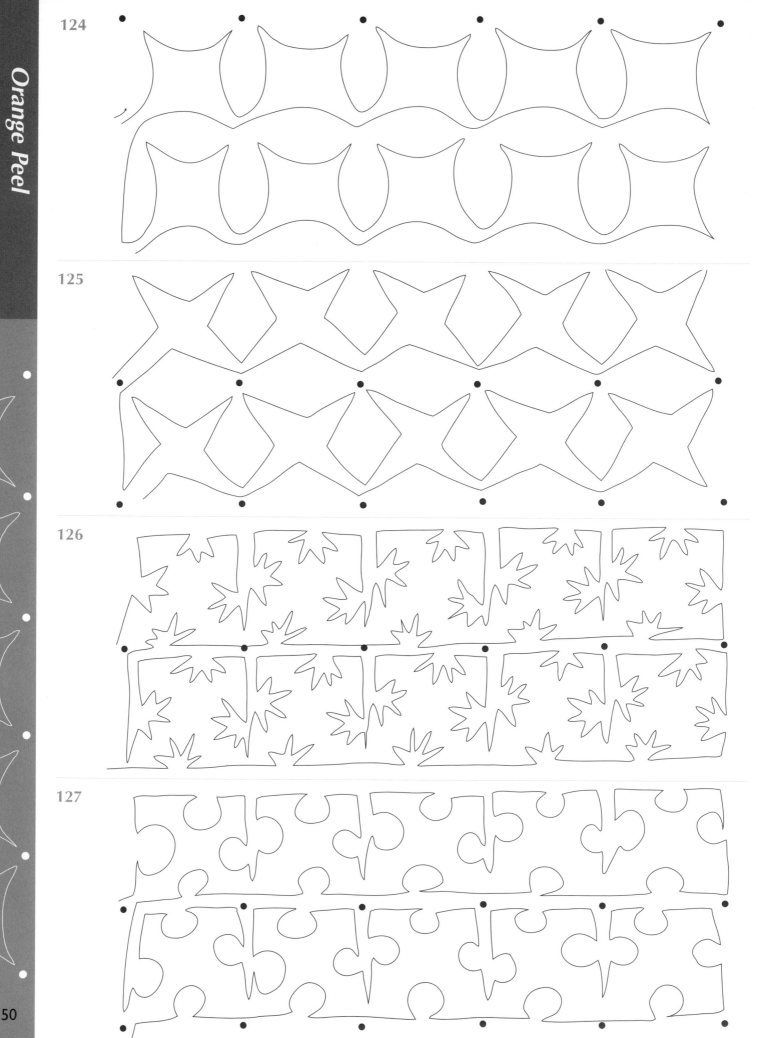

124

125

126

127

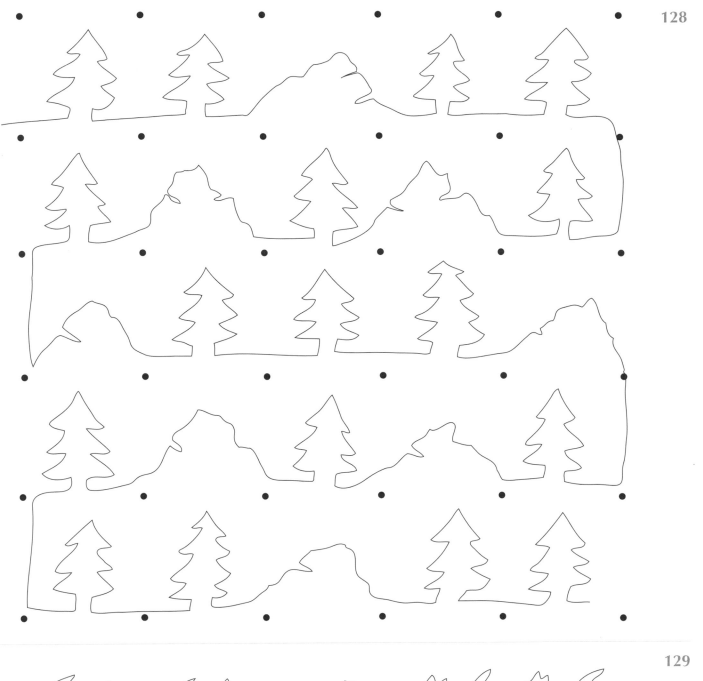

**130**

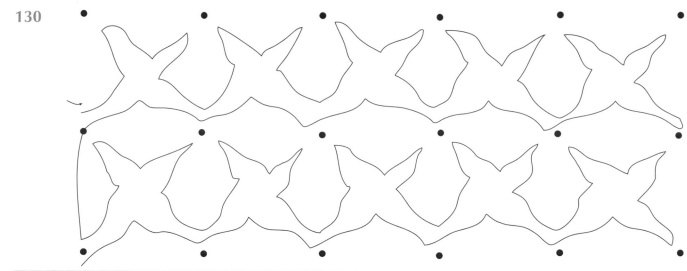

**131**

**132**

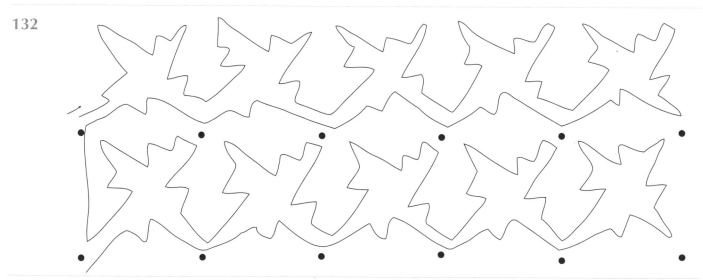

**133**

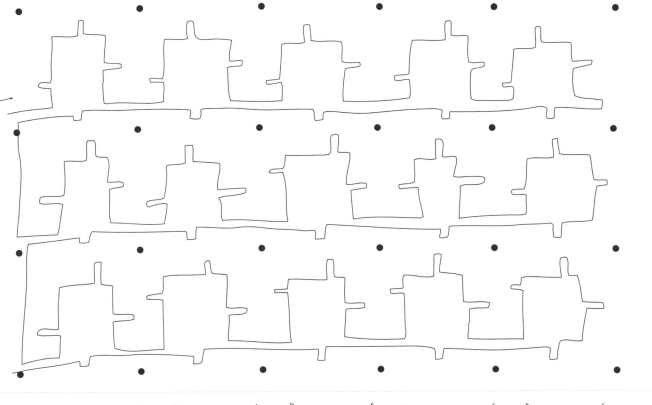

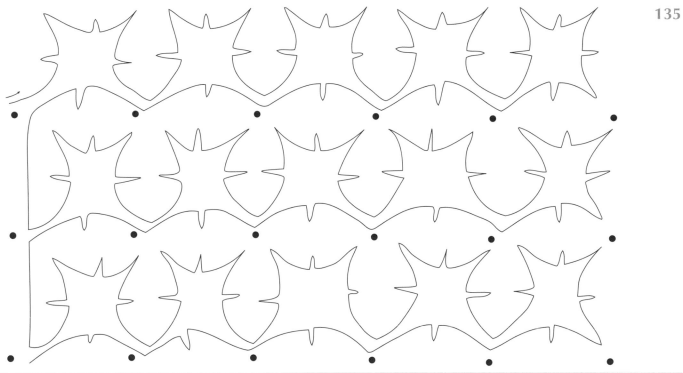

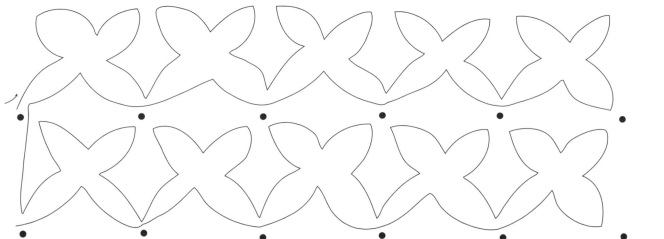

## About the Author

Laura Lee Fritz is widely known for her hand appliqué quilts and her fanciful wholecloth quilting filled with narrative images from the stories surrounding her life. Laura raises bluetick hounds and Navajo-Icelandic sheep in rural Bitterroot Valley, Montana, but slips off of the farm to teach quilting classes from Napa Valley College in California to her long-arm machine quilting classes at the annual International Quilt Festival in Houston. Drop in to see her quilting machine shop Houndholl'r Quilting, in a log cabin at the south edge of Missoula on Highway 93.

Laura Lee Fritz
Houndholl'r Quilting
P.O. Box 846
Lolo, MT 59847
877-779-2435

## A Word About Art

Being an artist is all in the practice of art. Those of us who make pretty lines attract people who value pretty lines. If we create bold, abstract lines we attract those who value that form. Folk art is a more spontaneous art form; we just need to make the story unfold. There are vast numbers of people who are attracted to folk art for its direct simplicity. Throughout history, quilts have represented people's lives, often expressing a love of story as well as love of color.

It is sufficient to practice your craft in an expressive way, and follow the path of just "doing it." You will begin to see the world with a greater attention to what it truly looks and feels like, and those observations will appear in your work. Now you are an artist.

# Resources

## Batting

**Hobbs Bonded Fibers**
200 South Commerce Dr.
Waco, TX 76702

800-433-3357
www.hobbsbondedfibers.com
/quilters.html

**Quilter's Dream**
589 Central Dr.
Virginia Beach, VA 23454

888-268-8664
www.quiltersdreambatting.com

**The Warm Company**
5529 186th Place SW
Lynnwood, WA 98037

425-248-2424
www.warmcompany.com

## Quilting Frames

**Flynn Quilt Frame Company**
1000 Shiloh Overpass Rd.
Billings, MT 59106

800-745-3596
www.flynnquilt.com

**Gammill Quilting Systems**
1452 West Gibson
West Plains, MS 65775

800-659-8224
www.gammill.net

**Handi Quilter**
76 S Orchard Dr.
North Salt Lake, UT 84054

877-MY-QUILT (697-8458)
www.handiquilter.com

## Threads

**American & Efird, Inc.**
400 East Central Ave.
Mount Holly, NC 28120

800-438-0545
www.amefird.com

**Superior Threads**
87 East 2580 South
St. George, UT 84790

800-499-1777
www.superiorthreads.com

**YLI Corporation**
1439 Dave Lyle Blvd. #16C
Rock Hill, SC 29730

803-985-3100
www.ylicorp.com

## Water-Soluble Stabilizer

*Solvy Wash-Away Stabilizer*
**Sulky of America**
980 Cobb Place Blvd., Suite 130
Kennesaw, GA 30144

800-874-4115
www.sulky.com

*Dissolve Stabilizer*
**Superior Threads**
87 East 2580 South
St. George, UT 84790

800-499-1777
www.superiorthreads.com

*For a list of other fine books from
C&T Publishing, ask for a free catalog:*

**C&T Publishing, Inc.**

P.O. Box 1456

Lafayette, CA 94549

800-284-1114

ctinfo@ctpub.com

www.ctpub.com

C&T Publishing's professional photography
services are now available to the public.
Visit us at www.ctmediaservices.com.

*For quilting supplies:*

**Cotton Patch**

1025 Brown Ave.

Lafayette, CA 94549

800-835-4418

www.quiltusa.com

Note: Fabrics used in the quilts shown may not
be currently available as fabric manufacturers
keep most fabrics in print for only a short time.

# Great Titles from C&T PUBLISHING

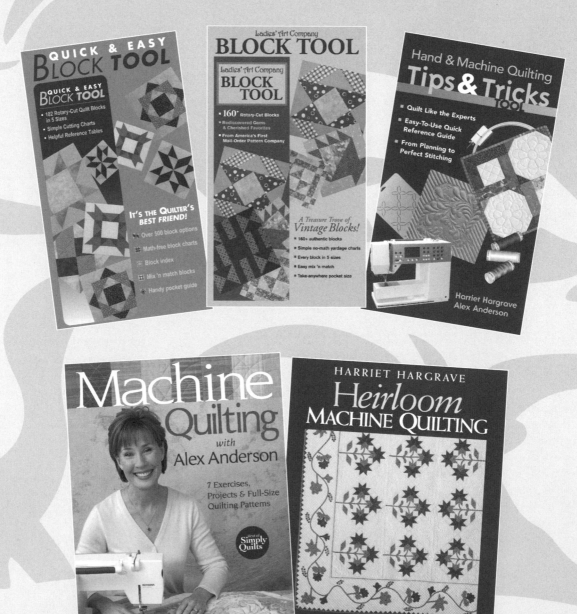